The | **Money**
Workbook

The | Money Workbook

A 30-Day Program to Greater Abundance, Prosperity, and Self-Worth

ROGER BRUCE LANE, Ph.D.

JEREMY P. TARCHER/PENGUIN
A MEMBER OF PENGUIN GROUP (USA) INC.
NEW YORK

JEREMY P. TARCHER/PENGUIN
Published by the Penguin Group
Penguin Group (USA) Inc., 375 Hudson Street, New York, New York 10014, USA ·
Penguin Group (Canada), 90 Eglinton Avenue East, Suite 700, Toronto, Ontario M4P 2Y3,
Canada (a division of Pearson Canada Inc.) · Penguin Books Ltd, 80 Strand, London WC2R 0RL, England ·
Penguin Ireland, 25 St Stephen's Green, Dublin 2, Ireland (a division of Penguin Books Ltd) ·
Penguin Group (Australia), 250 Camberwell Road, Camberwell, Victoria 3124, Australia
(a division of Pearson Australia Group Pty Ltd) · Penguin Books India Pvt Ltd, 11 Community Centre,
Panchsheel Park, New Delhi–110 017, India · Penguin Group (NZ), 67 Apollo Drive, Rosedale,
North Shore 0632, New Zealand (a division of Pearson New Zealand Ltd) ·
Penguin Books (South Africa) (Pty) Ltd, 24 Sturdee Avenue, Rosebank, Johannesburg 2196, South Africa

Penguin Books Ltd, Registered Offices: 80 Strand, London WC2R 0RL, England

First Jeremy P. Tarcher/Penguin edition 2009
Copyright © 2009 by Roger Bruce Lane, Ph.D.

Most Tarcher/Penguin books are available at special quantity discounts for bulk purchase for sales promotions, premiums, fund-raising,
and educational needs. Special books or book excerpts also can be created to fit specific needs. For details, write Penguin Group (USA)
Inc. Special Markets, 375 Hudson Street, New York, NY 10014.

ISBN 978-1-58542-737-6

Printed in the United States of America
1   3   5   7   9   10   8   6   4   2

BOOK DESIGN BY TANYA MAIBORODA

This publication is designed to provide accurate and authoritative information in regard to the subject matter covered. It is sold with the
understanding that the publisher is not engaged in rendering legal, accounting, or other professional services. If you require legal advice
or other expert assistance, you should seek the services of a competent professional.

While the author has made every effort to provide accurate telephone numbers and Internet addresses at the time of publication, neither
the publisher nor the author assumes any responsibility for errors, or for changes that occur after publication. Further, the publisher does
not have any control over and does not assume any responsibility for author or third-party websites or their content.

Acknowledgments

I wish to express my thanks and gratitude to all those who read the workbook with much loving discernment and support, and to all those who "worked the workbook" by doing the processes and gave me excellent feedback.

I also wholeheartedly wish to thank Marilyn Fiala Grossman, whose artistic abilities were put to excellent use in her loving service for the earlier editions in the cover and book designs and as liaison between the publisher and the production staff; Karen Baxter—our "KP"—whose computer expertise served me very well in the translation of this book into a living disk; Melissa Sones, who served as midwife in the birth of this work into the world; and Joel Fotinos, the publisher, who saw the importance of this book and who appropriately marked it "Territory: The World."

I especially thank my wife, Anna, who keeps me in gratitude, and my son, Jeffrey, who helps me know the abundance that is in each moment and who demonstrates daily the importance of the next generation.

Contents

Introduction

To facilitate the process of people's examining and altering their belief systems, thoughts, and values, I devised a training designed to do this, the Money Workshop®. We proceed on the assumption that we are creators of our own lives and everything that happens in them, and that we are responsible for our creation. We examine concepts of lack and limitation, self-worth and acceptance, giving and receiving, and the cornerstone of the individual's health and wealth: self-love. Some of the exercises and experiences in this book are taken from the workshop.

As you work the exercises and participate in this workbook, you may find your belief systems and values changing. This is all part of your growth into greater awareness of your power to create your life as you would like it.

A young man who had been involved in a successful family business and who holds an advanced degree in business was one such person who underwent this change. He had always felt that to work meant to work in a business setting, which, in his mind, meant the "corporate world." He also believed that security was to be found in a paycheck and a pension fund. Yet his experience was just the opposite. When his family business was sold, he entered the world of banking, where he began to experience a "vague uneasiness." He found that he was feeling more and more uptight, more and more stifled. He had always wanted to express the creative part of himself and found the security that he had heavily valued was making him feel less than a full person.

Through the processes found in this book, he was able to find security in his own power to give himself the life he wants and to make it okay for him to have it. He was able to leave the corporate cocoon and become a photographer. In his first year of business he earned more than he had as a banker. He knows he only has to tap his own powers to open up areas he wants to enter into as a photographer—whether in fashion, commercial, or portraiture. He knows that he only has to acknowledge his powerfulness, shift his focus from worry and concern to his power as creator to create what he wants, and he is truly back in business.

Also through the processes in this workbook, a young woman discovered an old family pattern that she had been following blindly in her life. As a child, she had always looked to one source for money, namely, her father—and not to her mother. As an adult, she had continued thinking that money would come from only one place. She also discovered that this pattern, in addition to her childhood habit of looking only toward her father for money, had been exacerbated by her father's doing exactly the same thing: he had looked to only one source—work—for his income and, in addition, only one kind of work—doing his music. This had resulted in his turning down all other kinds of work and sources of income and, as a result, the family's limiting pattern had been discovered. She was able to double her income within three months without, to use her words, "any conscious effort on my part."

Another young woman, a partner in a design firm, was dependent upon contracts being offered to her company and was seeking a way to expand, both professionally and personally. She had believed that circumstances of the business environment determined how successful she and her company would become. Through the workshop, she was able to shift "the base of power" from the environment to herself. She had only to realize that she was the only one who could determine her success. She and her company became several times more successful, being offered many lucrative contracts. She has since gone on in her design work in her own right and is now successful in Europe as well. She is also enjoying success as an artist, showing both here and abroad.

All of these experiences are the outer manifestations of many insights, gains, realizations, and self-empowerments inside themselves as they worked the workshop and the exercises. *These gifts are yours for the taking.*

This book is designed as a 30-day program to assist you in being in greater abundance and prosperity in your life. Following this day-by-day program, you do exercises that assist you in understanding and processing your fears and resistances and prior decisions you may have made about yourself and your life.

These chapters may cause you to pause and reflect and may provoke some decision making about how to live your life and the kind of life to live. Also, you learn how your thoughts, feelings, fears, or other "reasons" have until now held you back because they seemed to have the power in them that you did not until now know you possess.

In short, by using this book you discover:

- What you want in your life
- Whether or not you are giving it to yourself
- If you are not, why not?
- What you need to do to give yourself the life you want

In addition, this book teaches you how to:

- Give yourself what you want in your life
- Focus your attention
- Create positive "internal programs"
- EMPOWER YOURSELF!
- Love yourself
- Realize your self-worth

This book works the more you work this book.

I strongly suggest you "work" this book as if you were mining for gold. Just know that you are the "gold" you are searching for.

In your enthusiasm you may be tempted to do more than one day's exercise at a time. *It is important to do* only *one day's exercise at a time to benefit most from this book.*

The | **Money Workbook**

day | 1

The Check Exercise

Day 1

Please make out this check for any amount, payable to you, from you.

The Bank of Life

_____ 20 ___

Pay to the Order of _____ $ _____

_____ Dollars

For _____   _____

00000-000:00000000000-000:000000000000

Stop!

day | 2

About That Check You Just Wrote

Day 2

How did you feel writing out the check?

_____

_____

_____

_____

_____

_____

Did you make it out for the amount you wanted?

_____

How much do you really want?

_____

Now fill in how much you are willing to give yourself.

_____

❧ FOR TOMORROW

Please read the next day's material *early in the day* so that you have the whole day to do the exercise.

day | 3

People as Creators

IT IS NO SECRET THAT WE SPEND A GREAT DEAL OF TIME CREATING, WHETHER IT BE A relationship with the "perfect" person or the home run that wins the ball game with two outs in the bottom of the ninth. Our minds are continuously busy—"activity" being one of the main things to which our minds are attracted—but have we ever taken a moment or two and reflected upon just what thoughts our minds are focused upon? Is it something that lifts us and other people, or is it something that "knocks" them and, ultimately, ourselves? Are we focused upon fear, lack, and anything that limits us or rationalizes our self-defeat, or are we focused upon our growth, our strengths, and being of service to ourselves and others?

Let us take a moment to answer the question of how a person's environs are created. The answer is simple. Each person's thoughts are projected onto the world, and the world then materializes according to that person's thoughts. As a person persists in these thoughts, he/she becomes a reflection of them until the person manifests these thoughts. This is the meaning of the biblical saying that "as a man thinketh in his heart, he becometh."

We create the world according to what we focus upon; where we place our "attention" determines our direction.

If we have failure or illness or poverty in our lives, we may want to step back a moment and realize that the government did not make us poor or ill; society did not, even though it is an easy target for blame; nor did anybody. This means that there is no one to blame. But who is responsible? Each and every one of us is, for our lives. Do you mean I am responsible for my illness? For my failures? For my dire financial straits? For my anxieties about the future? With this knowledge comes the solution.

If we can create illness, we can create health.

If we can create poverty, we can create wealth.

If we can create failure, we can create success.

It takes less energy to create
positively than negatively.

The choice is ours to make.

At least four times today, stop everything and take note of your attitude, your thoughts, whether or not you are thinking negatively or positively. In other words, what are you creating inside yourself? Jot it down each time.

_____

_____

_____

_____

_____

_____

_____

_____

Day 3

✄ FOR TOMORROW

Please read the next day's material *early in the day* so that you have the whole day to do the exercise.

day | 4

The Antidote to Animosity

Day 4

WHAT ARE SOME OF THE ALTERNATIVES TO THE WORLD IN WHICH WE LIVE? A WORLD THAT is not defined by limits, a world where no one is subject to food, shelter, education, clothing, health limitations. It is worthwhile to note once again that "the world" does not give any of this to us. This gift each and every one of us needs to give himself—or herself—and as each does, the world becomes it, for it manifests according to our thoughts.

Another alternative is a world without war, without bloodshed. I have lived through two major wars in my life and I fail to see what we have gained other than more widows and shattered lives. War and terrorism in the world are a magnification of an enmity we carry against our neighbor, against people in the same town or profession. If we watch our thoughts we may be amazed and appalled at how we are constantly putting down people, even our "friends." This animosity we feel toward others originates in ourselves; some part of ourselves hates another part and judges it inferior. It is a psychological truth that whatever we do not incorporate into ourselves—and if we label it as "bad," we do not—we project onto others. Things we do not like in ourselves we see as "bad" in others. We also try to control what we believe to be negative about ourselves. Some control it by drink, others by gambling, or drugs or compulsive sex, and, in the extreme, by suicide.

Much of the world is based upon the need to control. A political or economic or religious system is thought to be inferior to another and so the "superior" country invades and attempts to preserve or superimpose its system. There is a large region of the world which shares the same religion but which wars amongst itself because of slight differences in its doctrines. It is as if they are saying to each other: "My way—or else!"

THE MONEY WORKBOOK

The antidote to this animosity, whether reflected on a large scale in wars or on a smaller one toward our neighbors, is to accept each and every aspect of ourselves. For, in the scheme of things, everything is according to plan; it is not "good," it is not "bad."

It all begins with self-acceptance. To "love your neighbor as yourself" is an impossible task without it.

A world in which each person is fulfilled, each person reaching his or her potential, becomes a natural by-product of this. It is not that our educational, political, and economic systems suddenly change. The structures that appear to govern us change.

As we change our thoughts to ones of self-acceptance and love and abundance, the structures made from these thoughts change, permitting these systems to accommodate our new potential.

I can just hear people involved in the world of business and commerce and other so-called "realists" dismissing the above as fantasy, as just so much utopian hogwash. I invite them and all others to conduct an experiment. Change your thoughts for a week, a month, and see how business improves. Go from "me, us, them" to "We are all in it together," from trying to profit from competition to everyone's profiting from working as a group.

Remember, we create our own reality!

Day 4

Are you willing to do this experiment?

Throughout your day, locate a stereotypic thought, saying, or attitude inside you. Write it down the moment you locate it. It could be, for example: "If I had more money, I would have more fun." "Everybody has more than me." "I would have more if so-and-so loved me." "I would feel better if so-and-so loved me." "Life is so hard." Jot down your thought each time it comes up.

_____

_____

_____

_____

_____

_____

_____

Stop!

THE MONEY WORKBOOK

Identifying and Acceptance Exercises

Day 5

A. IDENTIFYING EXERCISE

Complete the following sentence using your deepest, darkest secret about yourself or your most persistent problem. For example: "The thing I judge most about myself is always being late for appointments."

The thing I judge most about myself is

_____

_____

_____

_____

_____

_____

_____

_____

_____

_____

_____

_____

_____

_____

_____

_____

_____

B. ACCEPTANCE EXERCISE

Complete the following sentence using the information you just identified about your-self. For example: "I accept that I am late for appointments." Write the sentence ten times in your best penmanship.

I accept _____

I accept _____

I accept _____

I accept _____

I accept _____

I accept _____

I accept _____

I accept _____

I accept _____

I accept _____

Stop!

Day 5

⊯ FOR TOMORROW

Please read the next day's material *early in the day* so that you have the whole day to do the exercise.

day | 6

The Releasing Exercise

Day 6

Looking back on Day 5, say your acceptance sentence out loud while looking directly into a mirror; be sure to maintain eye contact with yourself. (It is best to remove contact lenses or glasses.) Do this exercise three separate times today, twenty times each. Be aware of any judgments or resentments that you may have created around this issue. Accept those also.

Please know that acceptance does not mean you have to like that part of yourself. Acceptance serves to release resentment and self-recrimination and, by freeing these up, makes that which you previously had judged that much easier to change.

❀ FOR TOMORROW

Please read the next day's material *early in the day* so that you have the whole day to do the exercise.

day | 7

Who Is Responsible for Our Creations?

Day 7

I<small>T IS NO SECRET THAT WE ARE CONSTANTLY CREATING</small>. S<small>OME OF US CREATE POVERTY</small>, fear, lack, and limitation, while others create success, health, wealth, and happiness. We are forever planning the "future"—daydreaming about it—only to discover that when we live it, it is, in reality, just a dream called a nightmare, and we wonder where we went wrong.

We are forever planning in our imagination what we are going to do when the time comes as it goes past.

If we take inventory of the hours a day we spend creating, we would find that fully two-thirds is spent in such a way. If we are preparing a dinner, we are worrying about how it is going to taste and look before we have put the roast in the oven. Why not just put the roast in the oven and leave the rest to our eyes and taste buds? Because the nature of the mind is to engage in activity and *the mind just loves to be busy.*

If we spend much of our waking life creating, whether in our imaginations or on paper in the form of writing or painting or whether we build model airplanes, and if it is in the very nature of mental activity to create, then who or what is responsible for these creations?

If I am caught by the police for speeding, a situation I have created by exceeding the limit, who is responsible for the creation of the ticket I receive? Is it the police officer who is enforcing the law? Is it the chief, who has issued an edict to get tough on such despera-does? Is it the fault of the town, which is desperately trying to fill its coffers by catching everybody going just one mile per hour over the speed limit? Perhaps it is the fault of the judge, who has just had an awful argument with his spouse and is angry at the world and cannot mitigate his anger by fining me the maximum number of dollars and points on my license.

Surely, the judge must have known the real reason I was speeding was that there had been an accident miles before, which had delayed me for an hour and I was just trying to make up for the lost time. The judge really does not know anything about cars, for surely he would have realized that because of the design of the one I drive it is virtually impossible to tell the speed I am doing without looking constantly at the speedometer; he would have fined the engineers and the company that made it, for they were, obviously, responsible for my speeding.

I think it is obvious from the above scenario that there are many people and situations I could blame, and all are equally "legitimate." But who really sped? The judge, the police officer, the car designer, or I? Who chose to ignore the speed limit? No one but me.

While doing the Money Workshop®, many of the participants have chosen to be late; all have "valid" reasons. The subways were running late; they could not find a taxi; they were in the building when the session started, etc. But when I persist in asking them why they were late, they found the real reason to be in themselves. They could no longer blame anyone or a situation over which they had no control; the cause was within themselves. Each person discovered that he/she was both the cause and the effect. This, then, presented a dilemma: for if we are both cause and effect, then we are responsible for both and we can take control. But how can we control our lives if we have been trained to look outside of ourselves, to the government, the doctors, to the experts, etc.? How can we stop passing the buck and control our lives? *Simple. Choose to do so.*

Knowing that you and only you are responsible for each and every one of your creations, choosing responsibly becomes the only intelligent action.

Day 7

FOCUS EXERCISE

Complete these two sentences and identify the three major areas upon which you focus most often.

1. My thoughts are most often focused upon

_____

My concerns in this area are

1. _____
2. _____
3. _____
4. _____
5. _____

2. My thoughts are most often focused upon

_____

My concerns in this area are

1. _____
2. _____
3. _____
4. _____
5. _____

THE MONEY WORKBOOK

3. ***My thoughts are most often focused upon***

_____

My concerns in this area are

1. _____
2. _____
3. _____
4. _____
5. _____

Stop!

Piercing Your Concerns

Day 8

Review your concerns. Put a line through the concerns on pages 22–23 that have to do with fear, limitation, insecurity, or failure. Looking at your three areas, what would happen if there were no negative concerns? In the space provided, create positively. Write a paragraph about each focus area without negative concerns; include the way things would look, sound, and feel like to you. For example, if you wanted a job as an executive and your concerns were around self-esteem, inadequacy, health and appearance, you would write: "I look wonderful. I feel centered and am in excellent health. I feel worthy of this job and handle each situation as it arises in my workday with confidence and self-trust."

1. _____

_____

_____

_____

_____

_____

_____

_____

_____

_____

_____

_____

_____

_____

_____

THE MONEY WORKBOOK

2. ____

____

____

____

____

____

____

____

____

____

3. ____

____

____

____

____

____

____

____

____

Day 8

Stop!

day 9

Identifying Exercise

Day 9

Let yourself have some quiet time today. During this time, thank yourself for the attention and interest you have been giving yourself the past nine days by saying, "Thank you, [your name], for the time and attention and interest you have given yourself."

Then fill in the following two sentences.

Something I feel guilty or embarrassed about is

_____

_____

_____

_____

_____

I now forgive myself for judging myself for

_____

_____

_____

_____

_____

❦ FOR TOMORROW

Please read the next day's material *early in the day* so that you have the whole day to do the exercise.

THE MONEY WORKBOOK

day | 10

Where Are You Placing Your Attention?

Day 10

BY DOING THE SUGGESTED EXERCISES YOU HAVE DISCOVERED WHERE YOU ARE PLACING your attention. Be honest with yourself: Was it a negative or a positive focus?

As we have discovered, we make our world from our thoughts. We also know that we are responsible for our creations. This means, quite simply, that *we are responsible for where we choose to place our attention.*

To many, this may seem like an abstract and even an absurd statement. Our thoughts seem to be "foreign" to us—that is, they seem to be outside ourselves, something over which we have no control. What we are really saying is that we are addicted to the same focal points and until now we do not seem able to control this addiction.

Nothing is further from the truth. We are able to control where we place our attention. It is as if we were to visit a city for the first time. We would find out about what places, museums, and theaters to visit, what interesting neighborhoods and architecture to see, what restaurants in which to eat. It is highly unlikely that we would visit a new city and indiscriminately visit grocery stores and laundromats (except, of course, if we owned them). Yet this is what we are doing with our mental activity. We place our attention (point of interest) upon something that is not very uplifting (the grocery store) that merely perpetuates our feeling worse about ourselves.

Let us say you have just bought a new car. You worry about making the car payments and paying for gas and its maintenance. This is a focus point of your attention. When you go to drive the car, this comes to the forefront to such an extent that you are not able to enjoy it, as you are obsessed with worry. You soon wonder why you even bought it in the first place. Subconsciously, you equate driving the car with an unpleasant experience and

want to get rid of it. You will probably pick a way to dispose of it that is in complete harmony with your thoughts: as you have been thinking that the car is not worth having, you will dispose of it in a way, such as an accident, that will leave it with its value lessened, even while it is parked somewhere. You could also have a more conscious awareness of your association of driving the car and concern about payments and its maintenance. You would then probably take the car back to the dealership where its value is greatly depreciated to match the depreciation of the car in your thoughts.

Any of these actions—getting rid of the car by accident or returning it to the dealer—does not stop perpetuating the paucity of your thoughts. The addiction of placing your attention upon a negative focus continues to look for its next "fix," another situation. You create situations to feed your addiction, for, in your life, your habit is primary.

How do you stop the addiction? How do you stop creating situations that have a negative focus for you?

You simply choose to do so!

A well-known biblical character, upon seeing a dog dying by the roadside, remarked to his traveling companions how beautiful it was. He simply had chosen to focus upon its magnificence and not its decay and death. Pollyanna-ish? Hardly. He was merely creating beauty and truth.

To re-create positively using the example of the car, we would focus on how good it feels to drive it, how easy it is to afford the monthly payments and its upkeep, and how blessed

Day 10

we really are to be able to afford and drive the car. *Yes, gratitude is the key to having and enjoying abundance on all levels; before it, the door to even greater abundance opens.*

If we focus positively upon driving the car and meeting all payments connected to it, driving the car becomes a most pleasant experience with few, if any, visits to the shop. Even if your income or money available is not sufficient, with this attitude, with this conscious placing of your attention, you create the money to support this. It can come through additional employment, through a gift or whatever way it wishes to match your consciousness of abundance.

❧ **READ** the material for Day 10 two more times throughout the day.

THE MONEY WORKBOOK

day | 11

As I Think, So I Am

At the end of this day, review the major events of the day and where you have placed your thoughts. What were your concerns? Ones of worry, fear, and lack? Pick out three thoughts that seem to predominate in your life. Write them down.

The major focus of my thoughts today:

1. _____

_____

2. _____

_____

3. _____

_____

Now ask yourself why you are placing your attention there. For example, if it is sex that predominates, ask yourself why. Is it because you need to feel needed and wanted? Is it because you are lonely? Is it because you need to feel okay about yourself? Is it because you have not yet found another adequate expression of loving?

List the reasons you are placing your attention in each of these areas:

1. _____

_____

2. _____

_____

3. _____

_____

Now change the reasons for this focus. For example, in the above, you would change lonely—which is an interpretation—to the fact of being alone. You would change your needing to be wanted and needed and to having to feel okay about yourself to the fact that you are already okay and that the world needs and wants you. Needing an adequate expression of your loving may become your job, your life, even yourself.

1. _____

_____

2. _____

_____

3. _____

_____

Stop!

day | 12

**Gratitude: The Gateway
of Self-Expression**

Day 12

GRATITUDE COMES FROM THE SAME ROOT, ETYMOLOGICALLY, AS THE WORD "GRACE" AND denotes receiving favors or being favored. When we live in the world we make, is it a favorable one full of that which sustains us on all possible levels, or is it "a cold, cruel world" where we have to scrounge around for the slightest thing? When we look at our perception of the world and the beliefs that create and reinforce that perception, we might be amazed to find that it is the latter view that prevails in our society. This book is devoted to examining our belief structures and changing our perception so that we can be open to what is, without the interference of our conditioned minds.

Gratitude enables one to be open to the universe, to its constant supply, resting in the knowledge that—despite appearances, including that of 9/11 and the anxiety produced in its aftermath—it is still a kind and magnificent world. The "cruel, harsh world" is no more; it is now a bountiful one, a friendly one where we are an integral, "nonalien" part of it in a nurturing, not hostile, environment.

Being in gratitude means one is deeply appreciative of what one already *has.*

When you walk around with this attitude you are not lacking anything but are living in the knowledge that all your needs are being taken care of. If such is, indeed, the case, you know that when you need something in the future it is there. If you are walking around with a reference in the future, it is there. If you are walking around with a reference point inside yourself of having your needs met, then you project that thought and, as the powerful creator you *really* are, you create your environment to match this thought. *Voilà!* It becomes a self-fulfilling prophecy.

THE MONEY WORKBOOK

When you live in gratitude you are coming from a place of completeness. There can be no anxiety, frustration, or depression about the "future." As your needs are met now and in the future, there is no lack, no "poverty consciousness" that say, "I need now because I do not already know that I have what I need for now and that when I take my next step I have what I need, too."

To live in gratitude is to live in true Abundance Consciousness.

Admittedly, it takes practice. Living in a consumer society that teaches us to be discontented with what we have and to solve that unhappiness by buying the latest products, we are constantly focusing on what we do not have now and what we will need. We believe we do not have the "ideal" home or lover or job; yet who was it that chose this for ourselves? We did.

Yet we pretend we did not, that it was just blind fate that handed it to us. So we spend a great deal of our lives waiting for the "ideal" home or lover or job—which can be a nice thing to do, except that our life goes by while waiting.

See the job as an opportunity to enhance your skills, or as a way of learning about that particular aspect of business or as a way to pay your rent so that you are not out in the cold.

When we come to realize that we created the job or apartment with which we are unhappy, we can choose to berate ourselves for our unhappiness and make ourselves even unhappier, or we can accept the fact that we did that. The acceptance of that fact clears

Day 12

the air of it and helps to bring in happier situations as long as our thoughts are focusing on more fulfilling ones.

The importance of acceptance cannot be stressed enough. It does not mean we have to love it or even like something. It merely means to accept it from a neutral space without judgment.

For example, if I am driving along and my car gets hit by another driver, I do not like it but I accept the fact that it did happen. I do not have to think it is because I am really a bad person or I need not have been driving around at that time of the night, anyway. Nor do I deny the fact that it simply happened. I merely take care of what needs to be done regarding my insurance company and getting the car to a shop that does good work. Acceptance is a neutral process, like simply turning a light switch on or off.

To be in gratitude brings about acceptance of what we do not like. If I am grateful to be alive, I accept the parts of myself that I do not like. Paradoxically, as I accept those parts of myself that I do not like and they become okay to have, it is easier for me to change and become what I had always wanted.

Acceptance of all parts of your life, together with the knowledge that you are a powerful creator, attracts a magnificent and wonderful "future" that was busy waiting for you to discover it.

GRATITUDE EXERCISE

Write down ten things that you are in gratitude for.

1. *I am in gratitude for* _____

2. *I am in gratitude for* _____

3. *I am in gratitude for* _____

4. *I am in gratitude for* _____

5. *I am in gratitude for* _____

6. *I am in gratitude for* _____

7. *I am in gratitude for* _____

8. *I am in gratitude for* _____

9. *I am in gratitude for* _____

10. *I am in gratitude for* _____

To assist you in the process of being in gratitude, a tape/CD titled **Meditation of Gratitude** *is available to give to yourself and loved ones. Please see the "At Your Service" section at the back of the book for information on ordering.*

Stop!

day 13

The Snap Exercise

Day 13

Think of something or a situation that you have been creating negatively in your life. Now snap your fingers or clap your hands, and think, see, feel, and hear this same situation in your mind, creating positively. Do this exercise as many times as it takes until you become proficient at changing a negative focus into a positive one. For example, "I would like to buy a house, but I feel I cannot meet the mortgage and the taxes, and I feel the house would always be falling apart." Snap and change to: "I am enjoying the house. I meet the payments and pay the taxes easily. I have plenty of money to decorate," and so on.

Complete the following sentences:

An area of my life with which I am not happy with is

_____

The positive value of being happy in this area is

_____

_____

_____

_____

Now make it okay inside yourself to have this in your life!

Stop!

day | 14

The Grateful Exercise

Day 14

Pick an object in your life that you are no longer in love with for whatever reason, be it your car, your wardrobe, your bed, your refrigerator, something that no longer pleases you. List five positive things about this item that you are grateful for.

1. _____

2. _____

3. _____

4. _____

5. _____

Being in gratitude makes you more receptive to giving yourself a change in this situation—i.e., a tune-up, a spruce-up, or even something new.

Stop!

day | 15

Acceptance Exercise

Day 15

When we feel guilty or embarrassed about something, we hold it as a judgment against ourselves. The way to release this judgment is through forgiving ourselves. The following exercise provides you with the means to forgive yourself.

Complete the following sentences:

1. Something that I feel guilty or embarrassed about is

_____

_____

_____

_____

_____

Now tell yourself: "I now forgive myself for judging myself and I now accept it!"

2. Something that I feel guilty or embarrassed about is

_____

_____

_____

_____

_____

Now tell yourself: "I now forgive myself for judging myself and I now accept it."

3. Something that I feel guilty or embarrassed about is

_____

_____

_____

_____

_____

Now tell yourself: "I now forgive myself for judging myself and I now accept it."

4. Something that I feel guilty or embarrassed about is

_____

_____

_____

_____

_____

Now tell yourself: "I now forgive myself for judging myself and I now accept it."

Stop!

day | 16

**Creating the Life You Truly Want:
Visualization and Programming**

Day 16

JUST BECAUSE IT HAS NOT HAPPENED YET DOES NOT MEAN IT HAS NOT HAPPENED. In the past twenty-five years, movies and books have portrayed an awareness of dimensions and events beyond the "normal" range of consciousness. The parameters of the brain/mind are being constantly expanded as science and medicine begin to understand its true nature. A leading daily newspaper featured an article exploring science's changing perception of the brain: it was no longer viewed as reaching complete growth as one completes the teenage years, but in people who were in their eighties and nineties, the brain was documented as growing nerve networks expanding outward. When the environment for people this age was not a stimulating one, growth of the brain corresponded and there was no expansion of the nerve network to incorporate and understand new and complex things in its world. Medicine and science have confirmed an age-old axiom: *Now is the perfect time to change.*

Knowing that we are responsible for the world we live in and that we create it, how can we create it to our advantage and to that of others? Two very important tools are visualization and programming.

In visualization we see exactly what it is we want. If it is a better job, what does it look like? What are the duties involved? What is the environment like? Your co-workers? What is the salary you wish? The benefits? Vacation and sick leave? How far do you want to commute? See the office clearly, even the color of the carpet and the walls or whatever is necessary to assist you in creating the feeling you want at the job! See your workers as supportive and helpful. If you wish a certain salary, see your employer joyfully giving it to you in grateful recognition of your abilities. See every aspect of your work situation in this light. If you are self-employed, you can create what you would like from this same

neutral space as if you were an employee. This serves to take the stress and strain out of your work that may have resulted because of your personal and emotional attachments.

Whether you are self-employed or not, you may also wish to take the part of your employer and visualize his or her needs. Perhaps a production assistant is needed? An administrator? A person with skill or expertise in a certain area? See your employees' needs and wishes. If you are prepared to fulfill them, a curious thing happens. Those wishes and wants you "saw" as an employee automatically are fulfilled when you fulfill those of the employer with love and devotion and from the integrity of your being. If you are going to complete the tasks being angry and resentful it is best not to do them. When you see your work as an opportunity given to you by your employer to progress and to grow, and not as a shackle, you willingly fulfill each other's wishes.

Beyond the dimensions that can be ascertained by the physical apparatus of the body lies one in which our wishes are heard and supplied to us. It acts much as a suction tube does: what goes in one end comes out the other. Therefore, it is very important what you put into this end of the tube for you receive whatever you have placed in it. This "tube" supplies our wishes much as oxygen is supplied. As we can create responsibly or irresponsibly and we are, in either case, responsible for our creations, it is best to create only what is truly needed by us. If you create being a movie star or being an outstanding athlete, have you also created being happy in that career? Have you created having the proper guidance and financial advice and acumen? If I want a car, have I ensured having the money to pay for its maintenance and loan payments? I could easily create having a car without creating the wherewithal to be able to keep it past the time the first payment is due. Therefore, *it is best to create responsibly.*

As the "tube" functions impersonally and puts out what you put in, you need to be careful as to how your wishes are worded. For example, if you want someone to give you a free ice cream, you might express it as an "ice cream on the house." Do not be surprised if it comes back to you in a situation where you are sitting on the top of a house eating ice cream or even having to lick it off a house instead of a cone. When you program be as specific as possible. Do not just write down that you want a good job that pays well. Write down the exact amount that you want and all the things that would make it a good job. Leave out nothing. As you write each one, continue the visualization process so that you are both writing and seeing your creation.

There is no need to wait until you have the program perfect. Continue writing and revising until every last detail is provided.

To safeguard further against creating irresponsibly, it is wise to begin the list by writing and then saying "For the Highest Good of All." This ensures that if you create getting a car, you have the money to pay for it. Or, if you program for money, that it would not come because your Uncle Harry was killed. It is a built-in protection. It also protects you the other way. If something is not supplied, it is because it is the "Highest Good" that it is not. If the car you programmed for does not materialize, it is because you might very well not be able to afford its upkeep and it would create a strain in your life or, perhaps, because of your driving skills or lack thereof, the citizenry is being protected.

Visualize as you program and program as you visualize! These are the keys to your creation. Attitude is what makes it open or not.

✧ **PLEASE READ** this chapter again before doing the exercise.

Then . . .

RESTRUCTURING EXERCISE

Complete the following sentence:

An area in my life that I am not happy with, and choose to change is

_____

_____

The way I want things to be is

_____

_____

_____

_____

_____ *, for the Highest Good of All.*

Day 16

Review your statements. Are there any objections in you to creating what you want?

Record these objections and restructure them positively. For example:

OBJECTION

I do not have enough money.

_____

_____

_____

_____

_____

POSITIVE RESTRUCTURING

I have more than enough money.

_____

_____

_____

_____

_____

Stop!

THE MONEY WORKBOOK

day | 17

Attitude Equals Outcome

As you were programming and visualizing to create your life, did your view of the world change? Did you find it friendly or still hostile? Did you stay in your conviction that you would not get what you wanted, that somehow "the universe" does not like you and would not give to you? And if you know or believe that you are supplied, can you receive it?

Do you feel good enough as a person to receive? Are you worthwhile or do you attach all sorts of strings to the gift? Did you feel that if you receive, no one should know it so that you hide your abundance? Did you think it would be taken away? Were you suspicious or were you open to receive? Did you believe in your creation or was it something which bears no fruit? Does the reality of what you are creating alter and change your view of the world, or is it still the same? Do you believe in and know your power or are you still living as an alien in a hostile environment?

Generally, when people program and visualize, they find that the first thirty to fifty times that they read the program, they do not believe it; the next thirty to fifty, they sort of fade out and experience a drifting sensation; and the last ten to twenty times they are in total agreement with the program. As people proceed on a daily basis with visualization and programming, disbelief tends to fall away quicker and belief comes in earlier and people also experience what they call "a lot of energy" behind what they are creating. Eventually, people begin to feel this "energy" all around them, which is another way of saying that they are in agreement with the program and are aware of the simple fact that they are creating their world, their environment.

Knowing and allowing the fact that the universe is benevolent to be central in your consciousness is the key to "Attitude." Maintaining and reinforcing this knowing by return-

ing to it enables you to increase greatly your "Outcome." This enables you to be open to receiving and not closed. If you are walking around and living your life from the belief that it is a hostile world that does not give you the time of day, the world acts accordingly and its gifts and the ones you programmed for lie just a quarter of an inch away from your outstretched hands. *The Universe does not make you a liar.*

When you are open and receptive to the gift, be sure also to be open to the way it comes. Many people, when they program or in their lives in general, expect it to come only one way. An example of this, which is very prevalent, is in the field of increasing income. Many people expect it to come only from a work situation and program accordingly. It is wise to let it come any way it wants to. It may come through as a gift, a loan, being a beneficiary, etc. Let it come, if it must, as "a thief in the night."

After my wife and I had programmed for our new house and neighborhood, we made appointments to see real estate salespeople. After spending an entire day with the salespeople, we canceled the next day's appointments on my wife's hunch to remain with the last one. After showing us two or three houses, he asked us if it was okay with us if he stopped at a house that, the night before, a person said he wanted to list with him so that he would be better able to show prospective customers. Little did the salesperson know that we would be the "customers." Many people who have partaken of the Money Workshop® have changed their view of the world, and either have been willing to let go or, at least, to experiment with letting go of lack and limitation and to reassert themselves in the world with the knowledge that *the Spirit supplies.* They found that when they bought a high-priced item that they had not previously allowed themselves to have the item was suddenly discounted, often as high as 70 to 80 percent. A leather jacket that sold for

$400 that their budget would not "allow" or that they had felt unworthy to have was suddenly only $120. Or they found that much more than $400 came to them when they allowed themselves to have it. It was as if the world had responded immediately to their knowing and had thrown in the additional bonus of enough money to buy it many more times.

When you expand your consciousness and let go of lack and limitation you find that the world has expanded with you. Actually, it was just waiting for you to discover that it is as big as you would ever want it to be.

Along with allowing the gifts to come any way they want, it is also important to let them come in their own time. If you have programmed for your new car to come by a certain date and it comes two years later, be grateful that it came when it did. If it had come when you programmed for it—which is a moot point—you would not have been able to afford it and would not have sustained it. Therefore, it comes when it does according to "the Highest Good." It is important to proceed accordingly and to continue programming even after your "deadline." Naturally, if it is for your "Highest Good" it may come before it. What is important is that you remain flexible and open to receive.

Rewrite your restructuring exercise from page 57 on this page. Write it in the present tense. Be generous with yourself. If you are programming for a new residence, for example, be precise and ask for all you want; if you want a patio, put it in; or if you want a particular area, amount of mortgage or rent, or the neighbors to have certain qualities, put in every detail.

For the Highest Good, I have or am:

_____

_____

_____

_____

_____

_____

_____

_____

For at least the next ten days, read (program) and visualize what you wrote. You may wish to do it up to thirty days, refining your program, if necessary. The more you visualize and program, the more this is integrated into your everyday consciousness. Before starting, you may wish to reread the text of Day 16.

day | 18

Giving-and-Receiving Exercise

Day 18

Make a list of three things in your life that until now you have denied yourself for whatever reason.

1. _____

_____

_____

2. _____

_____

_____

3. _____

_____

_____

Now pick one of the three that would strain you monetarily and psychologically, and go out and give it to yourself.

Now!

day | 19

The Acknowledgment Exercise

Day 19

In the space below, write down any and all changes in your view of the world, and any feelings that may have come up around giving yourself something that you had previously denied yourself.

_____

_____

_____

_____

_____

_____

_____

_____

_____

_____

_____

_____

_____

_____

_____

_____

_____

_____

_____

_____

_____

_____

THE MONEY WORKBOOK

Make a list of the main reasons you have used until now to deny yourself things that you want.

_____

_____

_____

_____

_____

_____

_____

_____

_____

_____

_____

_____

_____

You may want to carry this list with you to refer to the next time you find yourself wanting something. Anytime one of the "reasons" to deny yourself pops up, tell yourself it is not the truth. Then reprogram yourself according to this new belief by telling yourself, "It is okay for me to have what I want, and the world supplies it if it is for the Highest Good for me to have it."

Stop!

day | 20

Receiving Exercise

Day 20

Make a list of anything you want, and write in your best handwriting the following sentence for each item:

1. *It is okay for me to have* _____

_____ . *I am supplied.*

2. *It is okay for me to have* _____

_____ . *I am supplied.*

3. *It is okay for me to have* _____

_____ . *I am supplied.*

4. *It is okay for me to have* _____

_____ . *I am supplied.*

5. *It is okay for me to have* _____

_____ . *I am supplied.*

6. *It is okay for me to have* _____

_____ . *I am supplied.*

7. *It is okay for me to have* _____

_____ . *I am supplied.*

THE MONEY WORKBOOK

8. *It is okay for me to have* _____

_____ . *I am supplied.*

9. *It is okay for me to have* _____

_____ . *I am supplied.*

10. *It is okay for me to have* _____

_____ . *I am supplied.*

Stop!

day | **21**

Acceptance: The Key to Your Heart

Day 21

Acceptance has to do with allowing and resting in the knowledge that everything is okay and that things are just the way they are supposed to be. It means that I can accept other people regardless of their bank account, employment, social background, and class from which they came. It also means that whatever they are, *I* do not have to change.

Over the years, I have encountered many women who have married alcoholics and drug addicts just "knowing" they would change them. The only thing that changed was their marital status; divorce followed and the addiction patterns remained the same. Somewhere, these women had nursed the fantasy that they were "the one"—the one person in all the world that their now ex-husbands would stop for. They did not know that the only thing special was their husbands' habits and that the only thing that could make them stop was themselves.

When you truly accept you accept the whole package, the dirty socks along with the handsome face, the chipped tooth along with the beautiful body.

Sometimes when you accept things, you wish they were different. But if I wish my bank account were different, it is usually because I have not accepted the dollars that are already in it and have not yet come to the place where I am acknowledging what the dollars I do have provide in my life. Nor have I acknowledged and shown appreciation toward myself for earning and bringing to myself these dollars.

Appreciation is a very strong ally of acceptance. When a house or jewelry goes up in value it is called appreciation. When we increase the value of what we have and who we are, it is because of appreciation.

Day 21

With the ability to accept and receive what we have visualized and programmed for must come the acceptance of where and when it comes and of what we already have. When we accept a situation (or a person), we accept it without a need for it to change and with the knowledge that whenever and however it changes is okay also.

As we have discussed in detail in this work, we project our thoughts and desires out into the world and make the world accordingly; hence, the importance of where we focus these thoughts and desires. We find a similar mechanism at work with acceptance: *whatever we accept within ourselves is acceptable in others; what is not, is not.* I project onto someone else what I cannot accept within myself. Whatever I do not like about you, I do not like about myself; whatever disturbs me about you disturbs me about myself.

On a larger scale, nations, religions and groups of people cast what the psychologist C. G. Jung called "the shadow" onto each other. Wars, leading to further wars, which in turn lead to more, demonstrate that there has been no understanding and no acceptance within each nation or religion or people of those qualities and beliefs they do not like. It is a lot easier for me to bomb your house than to clean up my own.

Along with acceptance comes the letting go of having to be a victim. If I do not have to do anything to you before you "get" me because I do not perceive you as an "enemy," as no part of myself is one, then it is impossible for me to get hurt. When I get hurt, it is because I thought I was inferior or less than you and I experience what you do as a confirmation of this fact. Being a victim means believing that you have no control over your life. If that is true then there is no correlation between what you believe and the world and you can feel and desire without consequences in this world. Unfortunately, this is not

true for those who do not like to be responsible for their creation. Go about thinking badly about yourself and see if the world treats you well. Go about thinking you are to be "ripped off" and see if you find coins in the streets.

To accept every part of yourself and the world does not mean you have to love it or even like it. But it does mean that it is okay to have for however long you do and that you do not have to blame anyone, not even yourself, for it. If it is okay to have, then it is not surrounded by a negative creation of guilt and shame and this energy does not block the change as it does not surround it. It is said that *"acceptance is the first law of getting along with the world."* I know that whatever part of the world and myself I do not accept, it does not accept me. It is that simple.

THE GOOD, THE BAD, THE UGLY

On the numbered lines at the top of the columns below, write the names of three people well known to you. Under each name write ten qualities they possess, as indicated.

■PART ONE

Three people I know well are:

1. _____ 2. _____ 3. _____

_____ _____ _____

Ten qualities that I recognize and admire in each are:

1. _____ _____ _____
2. _____ _____ _____
3. _____ _____ _____
4. _____ _____ _____
5. _____ _____ _____
6. _____ _____ _____
7. _____ _____ _____
8. _____ _____ _____
9. _____ _____ _____
10. _____ _____ _____

Day 21

PART TWO

Three people (the same or different) I know well are:

1. _____ **2.** _____ **3.** _____

_____ _____ _____

Ten qualities that I do not like in each are:

1. _____ _____ _____

2. _____ _____ _____

3. _____ _____ _____

4. _____ _____ _____

5. _____ _____ _____

6. _____ _____ _____

7. _____ _____ _____

8. _____ _____ _____

9. _____ _____ _____

10. _____ _____ _____

PART THREE

Now go back to the names on the previous pages and cross out the names above each list. On the line above them, write your name. Then, go through all of the qualities you have listed—the good, the bad, and the ugly—and make it okay within yourself to have each one.

The qualities we see in others are recognizable only because we have them in ourselves.

End for Today

Power: The Knowledge of Peace,
Surrender to the Self

Day 22

MUCH OF THIS BOOK HAS BEEN DEVOTED TO DISCOVERING THE POWER THAT IS WITHIN US, the power to create our lives from our thoughts and desires, the ability to choose where we wish to focus and to create a positive environment both in the world and within ourselves. We have seen the importance of such qualities as gratitude and acceptance and the simple fact that *"attitude equals outcome."* We have learned the skills of visualization and programming to assist us in making a better life for us and a better world for everyone. We have seen that negative "concerns" such as worry, doubt, confusion, and fear do not have to be our concern as we focus away from these areas and choose to go into positivity. We have learned that we cannot be a "victim" of our own thoughts and feelings and desires unless we have decided somewhere within ourselves to be one for we know now that we have power over our thoughts and desires and feelings.

The thoughts and feelings and desires may not change in and of themselves. We may still have those negative thoughts about ourselves and, consequently, others and we may also have the same feelings. They seem to come and go. What changes for us is our relationship to them. Do we believe them or identify with them? Do we become them? Most of us have been graced with two arms. Do we walk around seeing ourselves as an arm? We are aware of them and realize their function and call upon them when they are needed, but it is highly unlikely that when a friend calls you up he or she says, "Hey, Arm, how are you doing?" We just do not have that as our identity.

The same is true for those negative thoughts and feelings. They are not you. You may be aware of them, but they are not your identity. For example, no one is an alcoholic. You are expressing alcoholism. This book has shown you that you simply focus away from what

you thought you were and your feelings, and start creating the real you. Actually, you reflect the real you as the "real" one was created perfectly.

If you have negative conditions in your body and your mind, you have a firsthand experience of just how powerful you are. Like most things, power can be used negatively and positively. You simply used it negatively and you are witnessing the results of that creation.

So be wise and use positively the power to create conditions in your mind and body that you want. Notice I said "create conditions in your mind and body that you want." They are not things that you happened to be stuck with, a victim of "blind fate." That makes you pretty powerful, for it makes you the creator of your own fate. I know this goes very much against the grain of what we have been taught to be true and of what we hold to be so, whether consciously or unconsciously. The Judeo-Christian culture of the Western world, and probably the Eastern half as well, is still being run from the myth of our expulsion from the Garden of Eden because of having eaten of its forbidden fruit. What this means psychologically for the human race is that we still see ourselves as being such sinners that we have been removed from the Source of life and are separate and remain so until we repent. This myth makes us feel like a "bad" person and also a powerless one, as we are no longer hooked up with the Infinite but have been expelled for our crimes to wander alone in the desert. This sense of separation, of lack, leaves us feeling adrift and powerless and without purpose in the world.

Nothing is further from the Truth. We are not powerless, not without purpose, but, as long as we perpetuate this illusion of separation, we persist in this. The truth is the opposite.

Day 22

We are powerful. We have the power to create our lives and the world around us and we have the power to use positively this power if we choose to do so.

THE "BEING A POWERFUL PERSON" EXERCISE

Three areas of my life that until now I have not been able to change are

1. _____

2. _____

3. _____

Using those areas, grant yourself the power to change them positively. In your best handwriting, complete the following phrases:

1. I grant myself the power to

_____

2. I grant myself the power to

_____

3. I grant myself the power to

_____

Stop!

THE MONEY WORKBOOK

day | **23**

Shopping for Labels

Day 23

Please reread the text for Day 22 and then do the following exercise:

Some negative beliefs and labels that I have placed on myself are

1. _____

2. _____

3. _____

4. _____

5. _____

Know that every belief or label you have listed about yourself is not you *but what you have chosen to express. In the space below list five positive ways you relate to the world and to others.*

1. _____

2. _____

3. _____

4. _____

5. _____

Stop!

⊱ FOR TOMORROW

Please read the next day's material *early in the day* so that you have the whole day to do the exercise.

day | 24

Mirror, Mirror

Day 24

Stand in front of a mirror. Make eye contact with yourself and say each sentence out loud ten times. From now on, do this exercise five times each day!

•

I am a good person.

I am totally worthy of love.

•

❧ **FOR TOMORROW**

Please read the next day's material *early in the day* so that you have the whole day to do the exercise.

**Being Present: The Gift You Are Always
Renewing and That Renews You**

Day 25

"Where are you?"

"I am hiding."

"I want to give you a million dollars."

"I am in the closet."

•

So many of us are focused into the "future" that we miss it when it comes. We have trained ourselves so well to look down the road five to ten years that when ten years show up, we are still looking down the road for the next ten years. We then repeat this pattern when these ten years show up. It is interesting that while we are oriented into the "future" we are concomitantly blaming the "past" for where we are today. A lot of this book has dealt with removing blame from the past and from people and yourself and prepared you to deal with the "future" by programming and visualization and the acceptance that you are a powerful and responsible creator. Let us now talk about the ability to be present, to "be in the moment."

This is not to be confused with the hedonistic pursuit of pleasure, with the belief, as stated in a popular ad that "you only go around once, so you'd better grab for all the gusto you can." Nor does it involve a person's being totally wrapped up within himself or herself or an attitude of "The hell with everyone else!"

Being totally present involves the same understanding as modern physicists have of the nature of light. It seems to contradict everything they have been taught and believe in. In fact, the very laws of physics seem not to hold, for light is both a par-

ticle and a wave—a seeming contradiction. The present simultaneously contains both the past and the future. *To live in the moment means to be present with all that is happening, self-contained in the fullness of your being.* There is no place for worry or concern, for regrets and second-guessing. It just means that all of you is available to yourself.

How often have you been at work or at school trying to concentrate and were unable to? Do you "drift off" as people are talking to you and focus into worry or something you have to do? Are you so preoccupied with career advancement that you cannot perform, let alone enjoy, the job you are doing?

So much of our society is programmed into "tomorrow." Tomorrow you will get the promotion, the job you have always wanted; tomorrow your knight in shining armor will ride by; and tomorrow the car that you have always wanted will be driven right up to your front door. What are you supposed to do today while you wait for tomorrow? Suffer and atone for your sins? After all, we all know it is always darkest before the dawn.

Why not move the dawn ahead a few hours? *Give it to yourself now!* Not tomorrow, not in three hours, not in ten minutes. Not after you get off the phone or come home from work. But *now*.

How do you make it okay with yourself to be present? Gratitude and acceptance are the keys. If everything in the past is okay with you and you possess the knowledge that whatever you need you have and whatever you need for your growth you have, then you are

not concerned with anything. If you accept all parts of yourself—all the aspects you have previously labeled "bad" or "inferior" or "damaged goods"—then your self-acceptance allows all parts of yourself to be available to yourself. This is the key.

The degree of self-acceptance determines how present you are. To accept yourself unconditionally is to allow yourself to be present unconditionally. That is it in a nutshell.

Throughout your day take note of whether you are in the present or tuned out, or in the past or the future. Tell yourself that you want to be present. Before the day is over, pick a phrase to help you stay present—one you can call on as needed. For example:

"Stay present!"

"I love you."

"We are okay."

"Attention, please!"

"Be here!"

On the line above, make one tailor-made just for you and use it the very moment you find yourself drifting or not listening or not being present. You can use your phrase at any time and when you are alone or with others.

Take note throughout your day of how you feel when you are present and when you are not.

Stop!

day 26

"My Momma Done Told Me"

Day 26

MANY PEOPLE GO THROUGH LIFE PRACTICING "VALUES" THAT HAVE BEEN HANDED DOWN from generation to generation but they are not appropriate to the present situation, if they ever were. Once, while I was playing with my son in the playground, a family of three children came by to enjoy the use of the equipment. The two youngest were separated by no more than a year, and the youngest one was wearing shoes that had been her brother's. I was struck by this notion of "thrift" and saving—something that runs very deep in the American psyche. What struck me even more was how uncomfortable the youngest child was and how difficult it was for her to walk. With every step her ankle turned and sometimes, her ankle not yet having the strength to support her, she tripped over herself as her brother's shoes were a year too big for her. Perhaps over the course of her childhood she may wear twenty pairs of hand-me-downs; this may save her parents $800. Yet if she should crack her ankle or suffer damage in some way these savings would be more than wiped out. Even if she did not, surely $800 is a small price to pay for that beautiful child's comfort.

If a friend or family member were to mention this to her parents, chances are they would be offended; after all, they were doing what their parents had done and were simply practicing a "virtue" that society demands. If pride can make the angels fall, surely it can make a little girl's ankle twist. Even though I really do not know that girl, I would hate to see that happen.

When we live values and practices and beliefs that are our parents' and grandparents' we are not living our own beliefs but are acting out of habit. Such habitual responses do not allow us to be present for ourselves nor do they allow us to respond to each situation anew; we respond as we always have and, as a result, we miss what really is involved in the situation.

If, by accident, a friend of mine steps on my foot and causes me pain, I would probably rub my toe and curse. But if I do this the next time I see my friend or the time after, then I am responding in a habitual manner. Would you rub your toe twenty years later when you see your friend again? Yet this is what you do when you respond to a situation in a familiar manner or live your life having inculcated the values of your parents without examining them for yourself. *I am not for a minute suggesting that you discard tradition; I am, however, suggesting that you make a careful determination and keep only that which works for you.*

·

Day 26

EXERCISE: A MOM-AND-POP OPERATION

Complete the following. It is okay to use any primary person in your life for this exercise.

The way my dad felt about money

_____

_____

_____

_____

_____

_____

_____

_____

_____

_____

_____

_____

_____

_____

_____

_____

The way my mom felt about money

Stop!

day | 27

Dear Mom and Dad

Day 27

Use this space to write an open letter to Mom and Dad (whether you know them or not) or any primary person in your life who helped to shape your beliefs about money. This letter is for you, to be shared only if you consider it appropriate.

Dear Mom and Dad,

It is now all right for me to be, do, and have the things I want in my life. The way I want my life to be is

_____

_____

_____

_____

_____

_____

_____

_____

_____

_____

_____

_____

_____

_____

_____

_____

_____

Day 27

_____

_____

_____

_____

_____

_____

_____

_____

_____

_____

_____

_____

_____

_____

_____

_____

_____

_____

_____

Stop!

day 28

The Reunion Exercise

Day 28

Reread the letter to Mom and Dad from Day 27. Is there anything you want to elaborate, or change, or add, or say differently? Do so now. Be generous with yourself.

_____

_____

_____

_____

_____

_____

_____

_____

_____

_____

_____

_____

_____

_____

_____

_____

_____

_____

_____

_____

Day 28

Stop!

The Grand Finale: Loving Yourself Is the Best Reward

Day 29

THE WORD *LOVE* IS, ACCORDING TO ERIC PARTRIDGE'S ETYMOLOGICAL DICTIONARY *ORIGINS*, related to an Old English group of words whose adjectival form is "loving." "Loving" simply means "fit for or worthy of love"—hence, beautiful, lovely.

Loving yourself, then, means that you consider yourself worthy of love; it means that you have accepted all parts of yourself and every aspect of you is okay for you to have. It does not mean that these parts are immutable and that you are "stuck" with them. You might not like it that you react angrily every time it rains. Accepting the part of you that does that does not mean you will react that way forever. But accepting it and making it okay allows you to let it go and change your reaction pattern.

Most of us do not think well of ourselves. We think we are "ugly," undeserving of anything, let alone love. Much of this can be traced to what we touched upon earlier in this book: the myth of expulsion from the Garden of Eden. This myth lies deeply embedded in the Western world's psyche and determines and undermines much of the actions of the human race. What this myth holds is that the human race has sinned by eating of the Tree of Knowledge and is condemned to wander around the environs of the earth until we realize that we are sinners and repent. Until such time, we are forever doomed to remain in hell.

Psychologically, the race has interpreted this to mean that we are "bad," that we are "unlovable" and are scorned and rejected by the power or powers that rule humankind. Religion then steps in and lays claim to having the only salvation for us. Only this religion, not any of its "competitors," can save us. But there is no need for this. The purpose of religion is contained in the word: it comes from *religio*, which means "to link back and connect to." Religion, thus, links you back to who you really are—a wonderful, beautiful

child of the Inventor of Being. All of our programming and conditioning goes to refute this simple truth. We are still walking around feeling like victims of circumstances, unable to control "blind fate."

The purpose of this book is to show that we make our own fate by our thoughts and desires and that we are powerful creators responsible for our creation. I must now ask a final and conclusive question:

DO YOU KNOW YOU ARE WORTHY OF LOVE?

If you do know, you are home, sweet home, to opening to the bounty and abundance that is this life. The irony and perhaps the joke of it all is that Reality wants to give us this love we seek. What we spend our life trying to get is really present for us from day one. *We just spend the rest of our lives being present for it.*

One thing needs to be added to the definition of loving that was given at the beginning of this chapter. The most important aspect of loving is that it is an active process. *Loving involves a continuous act of giving love. You giving love to yourself. What can be simpler than that?*

The gift of loving yourself spills over and out to your family, friends, and fellow workers and fills all. A pipe dream? Are you prepared to take the plunge?

THE "MAKING A NEW MOVIE" EXERCISE

Going into your memory bank of past experiences, remember a time when you had a disappointment. See it . . . hear it . . . feel it . . . taste it. When you get to the point where the disappointment comes up, change it. Give yourself the experience you wanted. See it . . . hear it . . . feel it . . . taste it. Do this exercise with three different memories:

FIRST

In my wildest fantasies what I really wanted to be was a

_____

_____

The way it would feel would be

_____

_____

The way it would look would be

_____

_____

The way it would sound would be

_____

_____

SECOND

In my wildest fantasies what I really wanted to be was a

_____

The way it would feel would be

_____

_____

The way it would look would be

_____

_____

The way it would sound would be

_____

_____

Day 29

THIRD

In my wildest fantasies what I really wanted to be was a

_____

The way it would feel would be

_____

_____

The way it would look would be

_____

_____

The way it would sound would be

_____

_____

Stop!

day | 30

**You Have the Right Idea . . .
Now Give It to Yourself!**

Day 30

In the space provided below list some of the qualities of Abundance Consciousness and what they mean to you.

_____

_____

_____

_____

_____

_____

_____

_____

_____

_____

_____

_____

_____

_____

_____

_____

_____

_____

_____

_____

_____

_____

_____

PART TWO

Complete the following sentence:

The way my life feels, looks, and sounds when I am expressing Abundance Conscious-

ness is

Day 30

_____

_____

_____

_____

_____

_____

_____

_____

_____

_____

_____

_____

_____

_____

_____

_____

_____

_____

CONGRATULATIONS!

YOU HAVE JUST COMPLETED THE 30-DAY MONEY WORKBOOK COURSE TO GREATER abundance and prosperity and wealth.

You have learned much and gained immensely and have grown tremendously.

To celebrate, give yourself the Money Workbook Award that you have worked for and richly deserve.

Please be sure to complete the blanks for your name and date.

Thank you for giving the gift of *The Money Workbook* to yourself.

THE MONEY WORKBOOK
Award

THIS AWARD IS PRESENTED TO

_____

for successful completion of

THE MONEY WORKBOOK

and for the achievement of greater

understanding of

Abundance.

COMPLETED ON _____ 20_____

Roger B. Lane, Ph.D.
_____

Afterword

You have taken an enormous step by giving yourself the gift of *The Money Workbook*. Congratulations once again! You have grown much, discovered a lot about yourself, and made a deeper commitment to yourself and to your growth.

I encourage you to keep growing, keep learning, and keep making a greater and greater commitment to yourself. One of the ways to accomplish this is to work the workbook. *The more you work the processes, the more they work*. People have used this book during its prepublication phase in various ways. Some people, after doing this workbook, did it every six months to a year. Others read the day(s) and/or the exercises that were most effective for them at regular intervals of a week or two, a month or two or more. There were those who worked the process or processes with which they had the most resistance; they would do this at regular intervals, also. Another approach was to do the workbook or read the day(s) and the exercise(s) that was (were) effective or those with which they had the most resistance at irregular or random time intervals. Some would pick a day or an exercise at "random"; many discovered that this was very appropriate to what they were going through. Still others wrote key points for their growth—often from the italics from this book—on index cards or Post-its and kept them handy and within sight.

Pick any of the ways of working *The Money Workbook* described above, or alternate among the different ways of using this workbook. Enjoy your growth and your discoveries and the gifts you keep giving yourself!

On the following pages I have included a list of CDs/tapes/DVDs and Workshops and Classes to assist you further in your process of self-discovery.

I thank you for giving this precious gift to yourself and encourage you to continue on the journey.

Sincerely,

Roger Bruce Lane, Ph.D.

At Your Service for Further Growth

The following have proven to be of invaluable assistance in helping people grow. Give yourself and others these gifts!

You may place orders for CDs/tapes/DVDs at www.cosmostree.org or by calling 212-828-0464. For information about Classes and Workshops as well as Trainings, Retreats, speaking engagements, and Meditations in your area, or to be placed on the mailing list, call 212-828-0464, e-mail spiritcentral@yahoo.org, or visit www.cosmostree.org.

CDs

Meditation of Gratitude by Roger Bruce Lane, Ph.D.
This CD is mentioned in *The Money Workbook* as being of assistance in moving you into a consciousness of gratitude.

Meditation for Health and Well-Being by Roger Bruce Lane, Ph.D.
A wonderful tape/CD designed to assist you in letting go of such negativity as worry, doubt, and fear that may be reflected as aches and pains in your body. Also available in Spanish.

You Are Worthy by Roger Bruce Lane, Ph.D.

A revelatory tape/CD that assists you in truly knowing that, contrary to the myth of the expulsion from the Garden of Eden, we are inherently worthy of the Truth of who we are.

Acceptance: The Key to Your Heart by Roger Bruce Lane, Ph.D.

A beautiful companion to Day 21 of *The Money Workbook* as well as to the many sections on acceptance. This invaluable tape/CD helps you know that you can accept all that you are, and therefore all that everyone else is. It's a must listen.

Success: What It Is, How to Measure It, How to Live It by Roger Bruce Lane, Ph.D.

An essential companion tape/CD to *The Money Workbook* that reinforces the Truth that you are worthy, you are powerful, and everything you need to be "successful" you already have inside you, right here, right now! Listen once a month and see what happens!

Have You Given Yourself the Time of Day? by Roger Bruce Lane, Ph.D.

A life-altering tape/CD that assists you in giving yourself the life you want.

For a complete list of the more than 125 Talks available on tapes/CDs by Roger Bruce Lane, Ph. D., each containing life-changing instruction on living in the Truth of who you are, please write or call: Cosmos Tree, Inc., 1461A First Avenue, Suite 182, New York, NY 10075; 212-828-0464.

Classes and Workshops

The following Classes and Workshops are designed to help you break habitual responses, learn new ways of seeing yourself and the world, and reprogram yourself positively. Many

Classes are available by teleconference. For a complete list of Classes and Workshops, visit www.comostree.org.

The first two classes listed below are the most popular and are essential to changing your life.

Everyday Evolution I is a ten-week series of classes that is most helpful in helping you change your inner script and decide what it is you want in your life, whether you want to give it to yourself, and then how to give it to yourself. An invaluable companion to *The Money Workbook*. Also available as a mini-class and in workshop form.

Everyday Evolution II is an intermediate ten-week series of classes for those who have taken Everyday Evolution I that builds on your ability to drop patterns and beliefs that limit your life, to handle what comes up for you in your life, to see every situation as being here for your learning, and to deal with every situation in positive neutrality. Also available in workshop form.

Everyday Evolution in your area. To organize an Everyday Evolution class or workshop in your area, call 212-828-0464.

Communication is a five-week series of classes that helps you learn to communicate directly, properly, exactly, and effectively. When this Class is over you understand how to ask for what you want in all areas of your life; more important, you will know that the place where this critical interchange really takes place is inside yourself. Also available as a two-week mini-class.

Fear, Hurt, Pain, and Other Attachments is a two-week mini-class that builds on the invaluable learning in *The Money Workbook* that you are free and that the power to create the life you want is within. Learn how to free yourself from attachments—to people, to status, to money, to anything that you allow to hold you back—all of which reflect attachments to inner emotions, feelings, and thoughts. You also learn the critical relationship between freeing yourself from your attachments and receiving what you want in life. (Hint: When we let go of attachments, we get more of what we want in life.)

The Money Workbook Course is a ten-week series of classes based on *The Money Workbook*. You learn, in a fun-filled way, what it is you want out of life and how to give it to yourself; to recognize your conditioning and to decide whether or not you want to keep it around. And most important, you learn the crucial relationship between net worth and self-worth. (Hint: There is none.)

The Money Workshop® I is a highly successful workshop incorporating many of the processes in *The Money Workbook* and going beyond It. It gives you the opportunity to move into greater abundance and positive self-worth and to give yourself the life you want. Expand your worldview. Empower your positive viewpoint. A must for those who want to give themselves the life they want. Also available in a mini-workshop and as a Training.

The Money Workshop® II is open to those who have taken The Money Workshop I and continues the work of that program. Here you learn to develop "goals" of positive neutrality and inner worth, and to allow rather than "achieve" them. The Workshop concludes with your making your own Tool.

Relationships is a two-week mini-class in which you learn how to have the relationships you want—in all areas of your life! It teaches you the essence of all your relationships and how to harness your own power and inner strength. Ultimately, you see that the only relationship you have is with yourself. A must on your resolution list for any year.

The TAR Workshop focuses on TAR, which stands for "Trust, Allow, Receive." In this revelatory one-day workshop, you learn to trust that you are supplied; to allow the Truth of who you really *are* to work in your life; and to receive the Abundance and Joy that are your true inheritance. This is a crucial companion to exercises in *The Money Workbook*— and goes beyond it.

Understanding the Spirit You Are, Part I is a ten-week series of twelve classes that is based on the popular video series Understanding the Spirit You Are by Dr. Roger Bruce Lane. This class helps you gain deeper insights into and apply many of the Truths brought forward in *The Money Workbook* and to go beyond them. Topics (and DVD titles) include Forgiveness; the Twin Towers of Acceptance and Gratitude; Living the Truth; and the Power of Choice. DVDs in this series are also available for purchase (see page 133).

Special Classes and Workshops

Classes and Workshops are available that bring some of the learning of *The Money Workbook* to parents-to-be, children, teenagers, and the elderly. Call 212-828-0464 for more information.

Trainings

Communication and **The Money Workshop® I** are available as corporate trainings as well.

Open Retreats

Retreats, which are open to the public, give you a much deeper understanding of key *Money Workbook* topics, including acceptance, forgiveness, gratitude, Abundance Consciousness, worthiness, surrender, asking for what you want, and loving yourself. Retreats are held in safe, fun-filled environments, away from your usual routine.

Accepting and Moving On. A very successful one-day Retreat subtitled "AMO Training: Do You Need Better Ammunition to Live Your Life?" If so, attend this Retreat. (Who among us doesn't need a bit of a boost?) Learn to accept the Truth of who you are and to use this knowledge to move on in your life. A great companion to *The Money Workbook,* covering some of the same territory and moving beyond it.

Living Spiritually in Today's World. This popular weekend Retreat helps you grow in the knowledge that you are responsible and that you have the power to cocreate the life you want, which is one living in the Truth of who you *are*. A terrific way to increase your learning from *The Money Workbook*.

More Tools You Can Use
DVDs

A lively Video Series, Understanding the Spirit You Are Parts I and II by Roger Bruce Lane, Ph.D., contains deep learning on such subjects as forgiveness, commitment, living in your truth, and abundance consciousness. Give this to yourself and your friends, either as single tapes/DVDs or as the entire series! It is a treat!

Tapes/DVDs in Part I are:

1. **Introduction**
2. **Forgiveness**
3. **Abundance Consciousness**
4. **The Twin Towers of Acceptance and Gratitude**
5. **The Power of Choice**
6. **Commitment: The Gift of Giving Your Self to Yourself**
7. **Living the Truth**
8. **"The False Self versus the True Self" Game**
9. **How to Sacrifice "The Sacrifice"**
10. **The Ego's Revenge: False Pride**
11. **The Only Real Question**
12. **Giraffe Consciousness**

DVDs in Part II are:

13. **What is Self Worth?**
14. **What is the Path of Soul Transcendence?**
15. **What is Meditation on the Path of Soul Transcendence?**
16. **What is the Theology of the Path of Soul Transcendence?**
17. **What Are the Teachings of the Path of Soul Transcendence And How Do We Use the Teachings?**

18. **Surrender and the Path of Soul Transcendence**

19. **The Final Surrender and the Path of Soul Transcendence**

20. **Living Free and the Path of Soul Transcendence**

21. **What Do We Do on the Path of Soul Transcendence?**

22. **What are You Doing for the Rest of Your Life?: An invitation**

Understanding the Spirit You Are is also a cable TV series in New York City. For more information, call 212-828-0464 or visit www.cosmostree.org.

Educational Publications

Tools for Living Free are easy-to-use (and carry), one-page educational publications that increase your learning on topics such as acceptance, gratitude, being present, creating the life you want, forgiveness, letting go of negativity, knowing you are worthy, peace, surrender, loving yourself, trust, and many more. Days 12, 16, 25, and 3/10/12 together are available as individual Tools for Living Free. "Step-by-Step" and "Try This" exercises increase the fun.

Receive a new Tools for Living Free publication every two months by signing up for our monthly newsletter, *SpiritCentral,* at www.cosmostree.org or e-mailing spiritcentral@yahoo.com. Order a complete Toolkit of more than a hundred Tools for Living Free by calling 212-828-0464.

Individual Tools for Living Free are free of charge when ordered through the website at www.cosmostree.org or by e-mailing us at spiritcentral@yahoo.com. Highly suggested are:

1. Acceptance: All That We Are

2. You Are Worthy of Abundance

3. Responsibility: Tag You're It

4. Responsibility: Tag You're It (Part II)

5. Being Present in the Moment

6. For-Giving YourSelf

7. Using the Tool of Gratitude

8. Creating the Life You Truly Want

9. You Are Worthy

10. Self-Acceptance

11. Being Present

12. Peace

SpiritCentral is a popular bimonthly newsletter that includes more fun-filled learning that enhances your growth. Topics covered in newsletter articles include being present, acceptance, loving yourself, creating the life you want, and living in the Truth of who you are. Sign up at www.cosmostree.org or e-mail spiritcentral@yahoo.org.

Speaking Engagements

Dr. Lane gives Talks the world over that assist people in knowing that they are inherently worthy, that they are free, and that they can surrender the negative (their creations) and focus into the Truth of Who they are. Some Talks are available with Spanish translation. For schedules and to arrange a Talk in your area, call 212-828-0464.

Meditations, Meditation Classes, Meditation Instruction for Beginners

Meditations and **Meditations for Health and Well-being** are offered at Cosmos Tree headquarters in New York City and at regional centers in New Jersey, Chicago, Los Angeles, Hilo (Hawaii), and in Mexico. These are offered year-round, including holidays, and are free of charge with a suggested donation of $5. Instruction for beginners is always provided. Cosmos Tree also offers visiting Meditations and Meditations for Health and Well-Being to companies, corporations, spas, gyms, old-age homes, hospitals, and hospice centers, and other organizations, institutions, and businesses that request them.

To bring a Meditation to your area, please call 212-828-0464 or e-mail spiritcentral@ yahoo.com. For center Meditation schedules visit www.cosmostree.org or call 212-828-0464.

Centers

Cosmos Tree centers around the United States and in Mexico offer a wide range of programs and events aimed at helping you move beyond limiting beliefs and behaviors to live the life of fulfillment of the True Self. In addition to Meditations and Meditations for Health and Well-Being, these include Video presentations and discussions based on the series Understanding the Spirit You Are; Classes, Workshops, and Talks via teleconference; and many other Tools. The New York City center has a lending library where you can borrow Tapes and CDs/DVDs. It also has drop-in hours when you can stop by and watch a DVD or listen to a tape/CD. For a complete listing of regional centers, visit www .cosmostree.org.

Gifts

Share the wealth and joy of self-discovery by giving *The Money Workbook* as a gift to others for graduation, wedding, birthday, or anniversary, or for no special occasion at all! This is a must for everyone in your life. And, yes, any occasion that you give someone *The Money Workbook* is extraordinary.

Master's and Ph.D. Programs

If you are seriously interested in continuing your Spiritual growth, education, and journey of Self-discovery—into the Knowing of who you really are—request a catalogue for the master's and doctoral programs by writing: Center for Religion and Advanced Spiritual Studies, Seminary Division, 1461A First Avenue, Suite 182, New York, NY 10075.

A Spiritual Path

If you are interested in pursuing a Spiritual Path involving the Sound Current and connecting to the Lord, God's Light and Sound within, please write Center for Religion and Advanced Spiritual Studies, 1461A First Avenue, Suite 182, New York, NY 10075. You may also call 212-828-0464.

About the Author

ROGER BRUCE LANE, Ph.D., founder and director of the nonprofit, tax-exempt educational foundation Cosmos Tree, Inc., is a graduate of the Wharton School of Finance and Commerce. Dr. Lane holds an advanced degree in theology and a doctorate in the combined field of Psychology and Theology called Human Services. Dr. Lane has developed a full educational program that includes Classes and Workshops in letting go of negativity and focusing on the positive; in exploring conditioning and deciding what, if anything, you want to keep around; and in the crucial relationship between self-worth and net worth (hint: there is none). Dr. Lane brings to Cosmos Tree a revolutionary way of teaching and learning using a Spiritual perspective in a nonsectarian way; participants learn to experience for themselves letting go of limitations, knowing their power, and learning to live the lives they want.

Dr. Lane's videos/DVDs from the series Understanding the Spirit You Are appear regularly on cable television in both New York and Chicago. Dr. Lane, who has been nominated for the Templeton Prize for Progress in Religion as well as for the Grawmeyer Award, has also lectured and assisted individuals via Meditations, Classes, Workshops, and Trainings throughout the United States and in Mexico.